WILLIAM AND WENDY

THE WORMS AND FRIENDS

BY J T SCOTT

WILLIAM AND WENDY
THE WORMS AND FRIENDS

BY J T SCOTT

Bumper the Bumblebee

Boris the Butterfly

Chris the Caterpillar

William and Wendy the Worms

Sally the Sparrow

Kirsty the Kitten

The Three Fish

Gertrude the Gnome

It was a rainy day in the garden.

William and Wendy the Worms

were watching lots of raindrops

dripping into their home

and causing a flood on the floor.

A raindrop dripped onto William's head.

"The rain doesn't seem to be stopping," said William.

"If more rain comes in

we'll have to do something,"

said Wendy.

The Queen Bumblebee flew down from her hive to see the worms.

"More rain is coming," said the Queen Bumblebee.

"You must leave your home right now.

Don't delay or you'll get washed away.

Why don't you ask **Bumper the Bumblebee,**

maybe he can help somehow?"

"Hello Bumper," said William.

"Our home is like a puddle of mud."

"Hello Bumper," said Wendy.

"The rain has come in and caused a flood."

"Why don't you come

and live with me?"

said Bumper.

"You could build a new home

up here in my tree."

William and Wendy wiggled up the tree.

"This is too high up for me," said William.

"We are worms," said Wendy,

"not bumblebees,

we don't live up high in trees."

Bumper thought for a moment.

"Why don't you ask **Boris the Butterfly?**"

said Bumper.

"Maybe he can suggest what to do?"

"Hello Boris," said William.

"Our home is like a puddle of mud.

The rain has come in and caused a flood."

"Hello Boris," said Wendy.

"Please can you help us find a new home?

We need somewhere warm and dry and not up high."

"Why don't you come and live

with me in the wall," said Boris.

"It's by the road,

but there's plenty of room

for us all."

William and Wendy wiggled into Boris's house in the wall.

"The cars are very noisy," said William.

"We cannot live in the wall," said Wendy.

"The noise is too loud for us."

Boris thought for a moment.

"Why don't you ask **Chris the Caterpillar?**

He might know what you can try.

Maybe he has an idea to help you stay dry?"

"Hello Chris," said Wendy.

"Our home is like a puddle of mud.

The rain has come in and caused a flood."

"Hello Chris," said William.

"Please can you help us find a new home?

Somewhere warm and dry,

not up high or noisy."

Chris thought for a moment.

"Would you like to live in my flowerpot?"

asked Chris.

"I have lots of friends who come and stay.

It's always fun and we play games all day!"

William and Wendy wiggled inside the flowerpot.

Lots of caterpillars were playing games.

"We don't mean to cause a fuss," said William.

"But there isn't room for all of us," said Wendy.

"It would be a squeeze," said Chris.

"If you don't want to live here you could try asking

Sally the Sparrow.

Maybe she can suggest what to do?"

"Hello Sally," said William.

"Our home is like a puddle of mud.

The rain has come in and caused a flood."

"Hello Sally," said Wendy.

"Please can you help us find a new home?

We need somewhere that is

warm and dry

not up high,

not noisy

or crowded."

"You could stay with me," said Sally.

"But my chicks are very hungry.

They might want to eat you for their tea!"

"We don't want to be food for your chicks," said Wendy.

"We need a new home," said William,

"and none of your tricks."

"We can give you some twigs

and you can build your own nest,"

said Sally.

"Or, you could ask **Kirsty the Kitten.**

Maybe she knows what's best?"

"Hello Kirsty," said William.

"Our home is like a puddle of mud.

The rain has come in and caused a flood."

"Hello Kirsty," said Wendy.

"Please can you help us find a new home?

We need somewhere that is

warm and dry

not up high,

not noisy or crowded

and where we won't get eaten!"

Kirsty pointed at her house.

"Why don't you come and live indoors with me?" said Kirsty.

"The humans I live with are very friendly."

"That is a very kind offer," said Wendy.

"But we are worms and we must live outside."

"Can you think where else we can try?" asked William.

"We need to find shelter until it is dry."

"Hello fish," said William.

"Our home is like a puddle of mud.

The rain has come in and caused a flood."

"Hello fish," said Wendy.

"Please can you help us find a new home?

We need somewhere that is warm and dry,

not up high, not noisy or crowded,

where we won't get eaten, or be indoors."

"Come and live with us in the pond," said the fish.

"We will teach you to swim all day long and all night through.

We are fish. That's what we do!"

William and Wendy looked in the pond.

"The water looks very deep," said William.

"We would drown if we lived in the water," said Wendy.

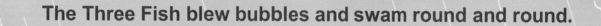

The Three Fish blew bubbles and swam round and round.

"Why don't you ask **Gertrude the Gnome?**

She will know where you can find a new home."

"Hello Gertrude. We need your advice," said William.

"Our home has flooded and we have asked our friends what to do.

Bumper said we could live in his tree,

but it was too high.

Boris said to live with him in the wall,

but it was too noisy.

Chris said to live in his flowerpot,

but it was too crowded.

Sally said we could stay in her nest,

but her chicks might eat us.

Kirsty said we could live indoors,

but we are worms and live outside.

The Three Fish said we could live in the pond,

but we would drown."

"Where can we go?" asked Wendy.

"We have come for your help because you will know what to do."

Gertrude pointed at the sky.

"Look! It has stopped raining," said Gertrude.

"Your home will be dry."

"Don't worry about the weather.

Some days it will rain and other days there will be sun.

Enjoy every day and have lots of fun."

"Thank you everyone for your help today," said William.

"The rain has gone and the sun is shining."

"We will have a cup of tea," said Wendy,

"and go out again tomorrow."

WILLIAM AND WENDY
THE WORMS AND FRIENDS
BY J T SCOTT

William and Wendy the Worms and Friends is dedicated to Mum & D2.

The moral right of J T Scott to be identified as the author
of this work has been asserted in accordance with the
Copyright, Designs and Patents Act 1988.

Copyright © 2020 J T Scott

First published in 2020

ISBN-13: 9798604831311

J T SCOTT

J T Scott lives in Devon surrounded by open countryside,
lots of castles, pens, paper and a vivid imagination.

She has also written the Sammy Rambles series
and created the inclusive game Dragonball Sport.

Sammy Rambles and the Floating Circus
Sammy Rambles and the Land of the Pharaohs
Sammy Rambles and the Angel of 'El Horidore
Sammy Rambles and the Fires of Karmandor
Sammy Rambles and the Knights of the Stone Cross

www.sammyrambles.com
www.dragonball.uk.com

Printed in Great Britain
by Amazon